MARY

CONTENTS

Copyright © 1990 World International Publishing Limited.
This edition first published in the US in 1992 by SMITHMARK Publishers Inc.,
112 Madison Avenue, New York, NY 10016

Designed by Bob Swan
Typeset in Perpetua by Face
Printed in Belgium

ISBN 0-8317-126 5-1

SMITHMARK books are available for bulk purchase for sales promotion and premium use.
For details write or telephone the Manager of Special Sales, SMITHMARK Publishers Inc.,
112 Madison Avenue, New York, NY 10016. (212) 532-6600

The Christmas Story

retold by Marjorie Newman
illustrated by Robin Lawrie

SMITHMARK

For Mary, the day had begun just like any other. Mary lived in the small town of Nazareth, in Galilee; and she was looking forward to getting married to Joseph, the local carpenter. Joseph was honest and kind; strong, yet gentle. She loved him very much.

Mary was sitting day-dreaming when suddenly she looked up. Startled, she saw an angel – Gabriel – standing close by. He spoke. "God is with you! You have found favour with Him."

Mary was terrified. What did this mean?

The angel said, "Don't be afraid, Mary! God loves you! You are going to have a baby son. You must name Him 'Jesus.' He will be great; and He will be called the Son of the Most High. God will give Him a kingdom – the throne of His forefather, David. And this kingdom will never end."

Mary tried to calm herself.

"But how can I be going to have a son? I've never yet slept with a man…"

"The spirit of God will come upon you; and the power of the Most High will overshadow you," Gabriel answered. "And the child which shall be born will be the Son of God. Elizabeth, your cousin, is also going to have a child, although she has grown old and people said it was impossible. With God, nothing is impossible."

Mary listened. All her life she had loved and trusted God. Now, she took a deep breath. "I will do anything which God asks of me," she said quietly. "Let this happen, just as you have said."

The angel left her. Mary sat for a while, trying to take in the tremendous news… Elizabeth! The angel had mentioned Elizabeth…

Hastily, Mary started to prepare for a journey. She would go and visit her cousin.

MARY

7

Elizabeth was married to a man called Zacharias, a priest of the Temple Church. Elizabeth had often prayed for a son. Now, as Mary came into the house and greeted her, Elizabeth was full of joy; for she had just felt her baby move inside her.

"How blessed I am!" she cried. "The mother of the Son of God has come to see me! And you, Mary, are blessed indeed!"

ZACHARIAS

8

Mary could see it was true — Elizabeth was going to have a child; and her cousin's words helped her to accept what was happening to herself. The two women hugged each other.

Elizabeth cried, "Let me tell you about my baby! Zacharias was in the Temple one day when the angel Gabriel came and told him I would have a baby son, whom we must call John. Our son is going to be special, Mary! When he grows up, he is to tell the people to be ready; for their Saviour, the Messiah, is coming!"

ELIZABETH

Mary listened as Elizabeth went on. "Zacharias wouldn't believe what the angel told him – we're both so old! So the angel made Zacharias dumb! He can't say a word! He has to make signs when he wants anything – or write on this tablet. But it's true about the baby! What God promises, He will do!"

And Mary said softly, "My soul praises the Lord God, and my spirit rejoices in Him. He has done great things for me, and holy is His name".

Mary stayed with Elizabeth for about three months before returning to Nazareth. In due time Elizabeth's baby was born. Her friends and relatives thought that she would name him Zacharias, after his father.

"No!" Elizabeth insisted. "He is to be called John!"

"But why?" cried her relatives. "No one else in our family is called John!"

They made signs to Zacharias about the name, sure he would agree with them. Zacharias pointed to his writing tablet. They handed it to him, and watched eagerly as he wrote.

He held up the tablet; and they were all astonished. Zacharias had written, "His name is John".

And suddenly, Zacharias found he could speak again. He began to praise God. Soon, everyone in Judea had heard the story, and were full of wonder.

"What will he be when he grows up?" they said. "Surely God is with this child!"

But Mary's baby was yet to be born...

NAZARETH

10

THE TABLET

11

When Joseph heard that Mary was expecting a child, he was puzzled and distressed. But he loved her too much to break with her. He decided he would have to hide her away, so that no one would know she was to have a baby before the two of them were married. The Israelites thought this was a disgraceful thing to happen.

But God sent an angel to Joseph, in a dream. "Joseph, son of David", said the angel, "do not be afraid to take Mary to your house as your wife. God's Holy Spirit has come upon her. She will have a son. You must name Him Jesus, which means 'Saviour,' because He will save the people from their sins."

CAESAR AUGUSTUS

12

Then Joseph was reassured; and he and Mary began to make preparations for the baby. They expected it would be born at home in Nazareth.

But one day, when they knew the birth would be soon, Joseph came hurrying in with worrying news.

The Roman ruler, Caesar Augustus, wanted to know exactly how many people were living under Rome's command. So everyone was ordered to go to the place where they had been born, to be counted. Wives would go with husbands.

And Joseph had been born in Bethlehem, in Judea. More than one hundred and fifty kilometres away...

There was no help for it. Joseph and Mary packed what they thought they would need for the journey into bundles. Mary made sure she had put in some warm swaddling-clothes for the baby. Then, with Mary riding on a donkey, she and Joseph set out for Bethlehem.

The road was long and hard. There were many other people making the same journey. With sinking hearts Mary and Joseph realized that the small town of Bethlehem would be full to overflowing. Where would they find lodgings?

Unable to hurry, they came to Bethlehem long after most of the other travellers had settled in. Wearily, Joseph led the donkey through the narrow, bustling streets to an inn. Mary watched as Joseph knocked on the door. From inside they could hear laughter and talking. They could smell food being prepared. But they were outside. Tired, hungry and friendless in a strange place...

Joseph knocked again. The door was thrown open. The innkeeper stood there. "No room! No room!" he said, and started to bustle away.

"Please!" Joseph's voice stopped him. "Is there nowhere we can rest?"

The innkeeper paused. This time he looked past Joseph at Mary; and he was very sorry for her.

"The inn is full", he said. "But there is the stable. The lady would at least be sheltered there – if you don't mind being in with the animals".

"Anywhere!" said Mary gratefully. She knew the baby would be born very soon.

And so it was that God's son was born in a stable in Bethlehem. And Mary wrapped Him in soft, warm swaddling-clothes, and laid Him tenderly on the sweet-smelling hay in the manger; because there was no room for them in the inn.

Then Mary and Joseph tried to rest. But soon the baby was to have His first visitors...

On the hills around Bethlehem, shepherds kept their sheep. The work could be exciting and dangerous. Not only did the shepherds have to lead their flocks along steep, narrow paths to the patches of grazing land – they had always to be on the watch for wild animals which might attack the flock.

Even at night the shepherds stayed with the sheep, wrapping themselves in their thick, warm cloaks, and sleeping fitfully in the open air by the camp fire.

On the night Jesus was born in Bethlehem the shepherds were out on the hillside as usual. It was a clear, quiet night. The only light came from the stars and the dull glow of the fire. The only sounds were the soft bleating of a sheep, or the restless movement of a lamb.

And then all at once, a bright, glorious light began to fill the sky, surrounding the shepherds with its brilliance.

Sleepily rubbing their eyes, they were suddenly wide awake — and terrified! What was happening?

Petrified, they hid their faces in their cloaks and lay shivering on the ground. And they heard the beautiful voice of the Angel of the Lord.

"Do not be afraid! I have good news for you, and all the people. For unto you is born this day in the city of David a Saviour which is Christ the Lord. And this shall be a sign unto you. You will find the baby wrapped in swaddling-clothes, lying in a manger".

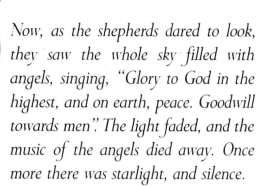

Now, as the shepherds dared to look, they saw the whole sky filled with angels, singing, "Glory to God in the highest, and on earth, peace. Goodwill towards men". The light faded, and the music of the angels died away. Once more there was starlight, and silence.

The shepherds sat up, trying to take in what they'd seen and heard. The city of David. That meant Bethlehem. Was there truly a baby born in Bethlehem that night who was the Christ, the Messiah, the Saviour?

The shepherds scrambled to their feet. "Let us go to Bethlehem at once, and see the baby!" they cried. Leaving one man on guard, the others raced along the paths, stumbling in the darkness, stubbing their toes, not bothering; only wanting to prove this news was true.

Reaching Bethlehem, they paused, panting for breath. Which way now? Bethlehem seemed to be silent, asleep. There were many mangers — animal feeding boxes — in the town. Everyone who owned a donkey would have a manger for it.

19

The shepherds began to walk along the streets, looking for signs that someone was awake. They came to the inn. There, from the stable, a dim light was showing.

The shepherds stood still, looking at one another, hardly daring to hope. Then, trembling again, they peeped inside.

And in the manger, wrapped in warm clothes exactly as the angel had said, lay Baby Jesus, with Mary and Joseph watching over Him. Softly the shepherds knelt to worship.

They told Mary and Joseph about the message of the angels. And on their way back to the hillside, as dawn broke and people began to be about, they told the good news to everyone they met.

And Mary remembered all these things, and thought deeply about them.

And when the time had come according to the laws which Moses had written down, Joseph and Mary prepared to take Baby Jesus to the Temple in Jerusalem.

In Jerusalem lived a man called Simeon. He was old, but God had promised him he would not die until he had seen the Messiah – the Saviour for whom the Jewish people were longing. So Simeon waited, and prayed; and at last God said to him, "Go to the Temple today, Simeon. Today you will find the Messiah there."

Trembling with excitement, Simeon made his way as fast as he could to the Temple Courts. He peered around at the throng of people. Which one was the Messiah?

Then Mary and Joseph came into the Temple Courts, carrying Baby Jesus. And Simeon knew.

Shakily, the old man went up to Mary. "Please – may I hold Him?" he begged. Simeon's face shone with excitement and love. Mary handed the baby to him.

Then Simeon praised God. "You have kept Your promise, Lord. Now let Your servant depart in peace. For I have seen Your salvation with my own eyes –

the salvation which is for everyone. The light which shines here shall shine for all nations; and it will bring glory to the people of Israel."

Mary and Joseph listened in amazement. Simeon blessed them. He said to Mary, "This child will alter the lives of many. But some people will speak against Him; and your own heart will be pierced with sorrow."

Gently, he handed the baby back to her. And a very old lady, called Anna, who never left the Temple, came up to them at that moment.

"This is the Messiah!" she cried. She thanked God; and told the people there, "This is the Saviour!"

Then Mary and Joseph carried out the ceremony of presenting the Baby Jesus to God, which the law demanded. And they made their offering of two turtle doves, as a thanksgiving. They couldn't afford the lamb and the dove which richer people would offer.

Then they took the tiny baby back to Bethlehem, to rest for a while.

ANNA

23

King Herod sat in his palace in Jerusalem and knew nothing of the angels, or the shepherds, or the extraordinary things which had been happening to Mary and Joseph. Until one day, wise men from a land far away in the east asked for an audience with him.

Politely, the wise men bowed low. But their words filled Herod with horror. "Where is the new baby king?" the wise men asked. "As we studied the sky, we saw His star rise in the east; and we have come to worship Him."

New baby king? To replace himself? Herod went pale. He ordered his chief priests and lawyers to search in their books. "Discover where this new king is to be born!" he said.

After a while they replied, "In Bethlehem of Judea!"

Craftily, Herod took the wise men to one side. "Go to Bethlehem," he said. "Search carefully for the child. When you've found Him, come back and tell me. I want to worship Him, too."

Unsuspecting, the wise men left the palace. They looked up – and saw the star. The same star they had seen in the east. It went ahead of them, leading them to the place where the Baby Jesus was. There it stopped.

And there the wise men found Mary, and Joseph, and the baby.

Mary and Joseph watched in astonishment as these splendid travellers from a foreign land knelt and worshipped the baby. They watched as the wise men searched amongst their treasures and brought out rich gifts for Him – gold, frankincense and myrrh. Gold was a present given to kings. Frankincense was burnt on the altar of the Lord God. And myrrh – Mary and Joseph shivered a little. Myrrh was used to help preserve the bodies of people when they died.

It was late now. The wise men rested for the night. And God sent them a dream.

"Do not go back to King Herod! He means to harm the child! Go home another way!"

So in the morning the wise men departed, and obeyed God's instruction to keep away from Herod.

Then Joseph, too, had a dream. An angel appeared to him. "Get up!" the angel said. "Take the boy and His mother, and escape into Egypt. Stay there until I tell you it is safe to return. For Herod means to kill the child."

BABY JESUS

27

Joseph woke with a start. He took a moment to realize what had happened. Then, hastily, he got up, stumbling in the darkness.

"Mary! Mary!" he whispered urgently. "Wake up! We must take the baby and get away. At once!"

He told Mary about his dream. Soon the donkey was saddled, their few possessions were bundled up, and the sleepy baby was wrapped warmly.

Then they set out in the starlight. They hurried along the streets of Bethlehem, with only the clip clop of the donkey's hooves breaking the silence.

God's warning had come in time. Joseph, Mary and the Baby Jesus reached Egypt in safety. And Jesus grew bigger, watched over, loved and taught by Mary and Joseph.

ZACHARIAS